THE PLOT AGAINST THE GOLDEN POT

(Or an analysis of the content of the Royal Treasury Chamber.)
By Trygve Gangnaes Jr

P A R T ONE.

Prelude or Overture:

What was happening over two hundred years ago during the time that George the English Finance King was plotting to keep control of the taxation income without representation of the American Colonies; it came to war with liberating aspects that ended with the Constitutional Republic of The United States of America. The prelude to this war was not just the cute explanation of the Boston Tea Party. It was a more serious issue than that. Our Treasured forefather and good citizen Benjamin Franklin had been an Envoy (or equivalent to Secretary of Foreign Affairs) to England, representing the colonies. In an honest explanation of why the colonies was doing so great and being prosperous, an unfamiliar term in European Finance, he explained that "it was because of their adopted "money system", the Colonial script, which was based on a regulatory measure of the Markers that was in circulation and was adjusted to the Gross Colonial Product summing up the value of Manufacturing, Trade and Distribution. This was a system that kept pricing predictable as no inflation was happening. It was also a system that was administered by a benign council meaning it was run by people with the best interest in mind for the colonists. I believe this information more than upset the King and his financial advisors as they realized that they were cut off from the proceeds and taxation of this trade between the colonies. King George had already implemented a policy for the colonies that went like this: "Though shall not use any money other than the British Crown."

Was this the real and more obvious reason for the Revolutionary war? ; The right to have their own monetary system?

A few years after the Declaration of Independence that lead to the warring conflict with England there were already monetary agents in the US that paved the way for in 1779, a ridiculous level of just what the colonists had avoided for "at any price"; INFLATION.

Today the inflation is built into the existing credit money system, as we all are experiencing on a daily basis. I am not going to get into the background and evolution that made this happen, but rather take the readers back in time and tell a story or two that should be of enlightening character.

History is considered a subject of facts and figures which may make it "boring" as a subject. It is also a rendering of historical events written by the victorious campaigners, Commanders or Kings, so that the other side of the looming conflicts never got to tell their story for posterity. Well, one of my missions, except for selling chicken coups, is to rectify that out-balance.

In particular there should be of interest the story behind the conflicts that resulted more often than not in: WAR. It may also be of interest to know that conflicts seem to be a specialty of ruling bodies of the past in their effort to conquer more land, position and power. I would like to define such conflicts as escalating to the degree where negotiation skills and diplomacy went way board and communication lines were replaced by bullets and cannon balls. What may be good to find out I think is "Who and What" was going on in the Initial beginning of these conflicts. Were there any other interests at play than the greed of controlling more land and people? A common denominator we may have observed even today beyond the fight to get an upper hand in the oil-economy is; I believe an underlying religious conflict. (About who is rightfully being credited of being the Creator?).

But there is a more senior motive behind these conflicts that dives into the money- or golden pot as I have called my story.

WARNING: Some of the angles introduced in this important manuscript will raise serious objections from certain factions of society even today, and some of them may go into a blind rage as I a non-scholar? having the audacity to exercise my first amendment rights (In the Bill of Rights, there is to be "no....abridging of the freedom of speech or of the press..."). But that happened in the old cultures 'of Europe and it happened to me in 1981, as an investigatory, documentary book was ruled; mainly historically incorrect (according to their "incorrect" version) or presented with an unusual angle even with documentation from all "reliable" sources. Revision of history is an ongoing thing as more and more information comes to light and makes constellations more easily understood. I have run into historians that grasp or clinging to the floskel "there is no such thing as historical conspiracies" and even "history is bunch of misrelated events."

But the United States has a powerful document that progressed and catapulted this country away from barbaric constellations and into the most prosperous country on Earth. It is called the "Constitution of the United States" and was adopted fifteen years after the Declaration of Independence—in 1791.

The subject of International Finance may have been purposely confuscated so the free people of the U.S Union would not get too many liberated ideas, and my presentation that from time to time makes leaps to connect up with the future, and is not as straightforward "as could be." It took me a lot of years to work the puzzle as that is what it is; a huge historical puzzle. I promise though that the data unearthed is far from boring.

With this I will wish you an enlightening excursion as you will get more than a glimpse of the dealing and wailings that is referred to as European and International Finance. To a certain degree we have all been a victim of this history and it is about time to lift several flakes of the concealing veil.

The Author, San Francisco, the sailor town 2015.

CHAPTER ONE: THE MEDIEVAL CASTLE

A man dressed in a black velvet jacket and baggy pants and a white ruffle shirt was bending over some accounting ledgers meticulously leading the feather-pen across the columns of the Royal

Treasury books. His long and gauntly figure had assumed a position where his back was curved in an awkward position; his bottom only supported by the edge of the high-chair.

The greenish light from the spring meadows that surrounded the medieval castle made by yellow sandstone never shined in this vaulted interior of the castle. The dust from the gathered treasures that counted several open coin chests was thick in the shaft of light that lowered itself from a positioned shaft high up on the wall.

The dust thickened air whirled all of a sudden into the Treasurer's nostril when he on an automatic exhale tried to get rid of the nose-itching. Then he slid out of his high chair in order to address the intruder that had caused the iron barred gate that acted as a door to swing open.

One of the members of the Royal guard had brought in a small round faced man. Next to the Treasurer he looked like a dwarf. He was quite bold headed and dressed in baggy merchant clothes. He handed over a letter of introduction from the Prince himself and while the Treasurer scrutinized the inconsistent handwriting of the

Prince, a broad smile spread over the face of the visitor when his eyes fell on the two still open treasury chests. The newly arrived was an expert in the discipline of chess and European coins; knowledge he had acquired when attending the yearly market in Brussels where merchants from different countries met to exchange wares and thus money.

The Treasurer gave the small man access to the rare coin department that consisted of different drawers in an old scrolled cover writing desk at the farthest corner of the old prison cell that had been turned into a Treasury Chamber. At this point the barred gate had been locked behind them with the guard still inside on post watching the small man while the Treasurer went back to his figures.

A fly that had been previously located at the top of the ceiling where the jointed vault-curves came together was now peeping over the shoulder of the Treasurer –a trained eye could decipher his fancy handwriting of the different columns as:

CHAPTER TWO: BUSINESS AS UNUSUAL.

RENTAL of soldiers to foreign powers of War.-this column had a subheading that read:

--The colonies of Americo

--The Prussian-Austrian conflict

--Spanish settlements and--Corsican kick-backs.

The fly recorded the last account as something beyond comprehension. *"What did the Corsicans have to do with Royal accounting in a Germanic Duchy?"*

The harbor of de Cargese-Porto was not as frequently visited by the caper-ships as a'Ajaccio, which was the main port for the landing of "rescued" goods and along with the ships that "had been found" floating and "abandoned" in the Bay of Biscayne. As a rule; no survivors of the crew was ever found on these ships after they had been through stormy weather. That harbor below the mighty mountain Mont Cento was a hold-out for ruffians.

There was another factor though that was spoken of than the storms that struck the waters of Biscayne and that was the sudden strike from the Caper Captains; a sophisticated name for the Captain of a ship with Pirates, that roamed and terrorized the Area. Many a crew of the conquered British ships that was not struck down in an uneven battle ended their seamen's lives tied to a rock or heavy object of no value—sometimes a rusty canon ball at the bottom of the Bay. Lucky survivors had escaped that wet grave and thus lived to tell their stories.

The hilly and mountainous Corsican Island that belonged to France but was located closer to the Italian coast was ruled by a mix of refugees from the French system of Justice and renegades of different kinds, after the English King George the III-rd had given it up. These had found a safe haven and thus another chance of participating in those "adventurous" missions that could have a successful outcome whenever they left the Corsican harbors. One of these men that were going to make European history in more than one way came from Ajaccio in order to enroll in the French Cadet School in 1779 as a ten year old about the same time as the Rothschild Patriarch entered the vaults of the Hessian Duchy. This young boy that would later rule most of Western Europe on the path to destruction with countless of lives lost was Napoleon Bonaparte.

The British Crown had grown weary of the prospect of bringing real money to the main Campaigner against Napoleon in Spain. His name became later Duke of Wellington and as a successful warrior-General, was given land and titles by the British Monarch –on the Irish isle. The Sea across the Biscayne was not a safe place to transport military funding in gold as the Napoleonic blockade had proved effective.

Meanwhile the Rothschild Patriarch had fostered five sons and several daughters. One of the sons, the third eldest, Nathan had travelled to England and set up shop; in the textile industry. His city of choice after other groups of German merchants had been driven out of Liverpool, a convenient harbor on the West Coast, became Manchester located a bit further inland. Nathan Rothschild was at that point not well situated financially but managed to raise money *from the family and he started to buy direct from the factories at first in Manchester and then later*

Liverpool and since he was the middle man as well as the exporting merchant to the Germanic States and cities he landed some great profits. This merchant venture was just the beginning to even more profitable ventures.

Meanwhile his dad had graduated from advisor to the Prince of Hessian on rare coins to giving or granting small loans to the royalties. This was a long way from buying and selling junk in that old business in Frankfurt. There had been an intermediate step however where the Patriarch, knowing the coin business had bought up different currencies that was left with the merchants at the Fairs. So as such he had trodden his first shoes as a Wechselerer or Money Changer. This is how he had increased his capital to get into the "government loan business" we believe. They started with smaller loans at first and then as his good reputation got around larger and larger loans even to foreign countries as Austria-Hungary and France took place.

Let me dwell right here with the scenario described. Originally and traditionally Royalties or small governments had to have money available before they could spend it—that is basic household economics. Now where did the Royalties get the money from in the first place?; mainly through the taxation of the people.

An historical event comes to mind—the Polish peasant revolt against the Lords that owed the land that had been acquired by conquering with the help of rented/hired warriors or mercenaries went on a far-reaching revolt. So what was the reason or cause of the Polish Revolt----it was burdensome or aggressive tax collection! These advanced tax collectors were part of a group of people that had moved in from the Eastern Europe of which many may have been refugees. This one of several happened around the year 1500 and when Martin Luther THE REFORMER came on the scene. In northern Europe there had been another group that had had that function of collecting taxes. Their other function was to record history from their abode in the Holy Roman Church's convents or monasteries. They were the monks.

To draw a parallel to the Hessian Princes and the Polish Land Lords and up to today's situation where the politicians decides on expenses needed that there is no coverage for in the Treasury. (Many countries has abandoned the basic accounting procedures of the Treasury and replaced it with what is referred to as the "National banking system" which is mainly a consortium of a fairly new breed in history called financiers. These are a group of private bankers that has claws in the finance systems "treasury accounts" of several western countries. The European bank in Frankfurt (1996-97), the Swedish "Riks-banken" (1685) and of course the Federal Reserve (1913) are such groups that makes available the money to greedy politicians and Princes of the past, that wanted to spend before the money was available; at higher and higher stakes.

Recent examples of spending greed besides Washington DC happened in Iceland (a Nordic Viking country) and Greece; both these countries are/were members of the European Union and had adopted the Euro currency. Eyewitnesses that know the troopers on the ground states that this all came about with offering credit cards even to the youngsters starting college. Several other EU-countries as Ireland, Denmark and Spain are battling similar problems of political overspending. One serious aspect of the Ukrainian conflict I believe is to be found in the fact that this newly established free country that graduated from the yoke of communism are reluctant to go into another "big brother" relationship. Ukraine has a lot of assets, Including agricultural land and still have a memory of what happened to them during the communist empire era where these assets were frozen by that government to control potential rebels on the subject of making food scarce—millions of Ukrainians succumbed in that created famine. They have also showed the world during one of the free elections in the early 2000, that they have this stubborn will of staying independent and not go into another coalition or Union. In November of 2005, the free people of Ukraine met in that plaza in Kiev, where that bronze statue of the symbol for the communist rebellion were Judas Iscariot standing there with his right hand fist raised defiantly towards the sky. This was witnessed by a Danish Diplomat, Henning Kehlet and recorded in his book Russian Chronicles, from 1919.He had been on a mission of repatriation of Bulgarian troops trapped behind the Bolshevik front. One can interpret this statue as a symbol the way one wants, however I believe it was definitely anti-Christian undertones connected to its presence.

The Ukrainians had elected their Presidential candidate and when faced with a candidate not of their choice they participated on that same plaza in a silent protest and stand off for close to 3 weeks in November winter weather. The armed guards were waiting for an occasion to shoot, but a few provocateurs were fast taken care of by the crowd, and eventually the guards military/police joined the protesters and thus they ended up getting the candidate they knew they had elected.

I need to back track to the time we were looking into—before and after the French Revolution and the Napoleonic Wars. One country that had been siding with Napoleon was Denmark. We may remember the onslaught on Copenhagen by Admiral Horatio Nelson that cannonaded the city and some of their ancient buildings.

Bottom line; Denmark was in real financial trouble. At the time they were considered bankrupt, and didn't have money to rebuild and for other vital expenses so they invited in a group of financiers, that took control of the Danish national bank or treasury of 1814. The citizens were grateful and gave these men first mortgage of the buildings they financed!!

NOTE: Today countries are not being declared bankrupt, as there always is external finance institution willing to lend them a hand.

Nathan's next adventure was to buy the textile materials and even the coloring for the clothes (then just bypassing part of the manufacturing business) and place a larger order at reduced price where he found a manufacturer that had free capacity on his machines. Clever way of conducting "business" of course as this way he could sell with double to triple profit. He could also of course sell much cheaper than the competition and controlling more and more of the market and thus create wealth in different ways!!

This way of conducting business he would place himself into smaller monopolies where he could control and be in the position to buy up competition.

NOTE: A Monopoly is an unchallenged business situation that has gotten rid of competition to the tune of a future Rockefeller statement<: "Competition is a sin" and I believe this was referred to when he bought up oilrigs as he could squeeze out the competition to the inception of Standard Oil by controlling/owning the transport lines (the railroads).

This successful son having relocated from Frankfurt to England was the 3rd oldest of the five brothers. The next oldest son had traveled to Austria to establish enterprise there, while the 4th oldest had been sent to" Paris" which was now the domain of the Bonaparte regime. So when Wellington, later Duke Wellington, needed a safe way to transport gold-coins, the two Rothschild brothers Nathan and James (Jacob) got into business together across enemy-lines and came up with a solution.

The Textile Industry was just a minor game for the Rothschild-family as the new building of rail-roads became the "new game in town". This venture made it necessary and more feasible to operate across the borders, as with the moving of money a lot faster than with horse and carriage.

CHAPTER THREE:

FROM JUNK BUSINESS TO RARE COINS TO WECHSELERER (BANKERS) AND TO THE TRANSPORT OF GOLD BUSINESS:

The year was 1806, and Napoleon was on the move and his first target was I believe the Germanic Duchies and City States with some exceptions. The Prince of Hessen had left the treasures into the hands of the Rothschild Patriarch and left for Royal family in Denmark.

The Prince let the Patriarch get free reign of the money and was happy with:

One: Having the treasure in good hands. He was by now a trusted MAN IN THE MONEY-BUSINESS>

Two: The promise of a small return on the money if the Patriarch was allowed to reinvest some of that wealth, which the Prince allowed as proceeds from their administration of their wealth would then find its way to Copenhagen in "double bottomed" carriages. I don't think there is any record of obvious reasons of what percentage of what amount that Maier Amschel thus shipped abroad. The Prince that had been separated from his wealth was most likely happy with any amount that found its way to his exile in Copenhagen. So there was no monkey business connected to this if you know what I mean. He actually safeguarded the wealth of the Prince and allotted some interest for the use of the money. An undisclosed amount was shipped to set up his sons in business.

The obvious fact that any historian may have been left out was the fact that Jacob-James Rothschild was in Paris that was ruled by Napoleon when the East Indian Company was ready to sell Gold for over 800,000 pound sterling (close to 10 million dollars at the time) to England. The British Government needed a large part of this money to be sent to General Wellington for his war campaign against the Napoleon in Spain. Napoleon was ready to place his brother Joseph on the Spanish throne.

He, the 4th oldest and next youngest son of the Patriarch, carried out this assignment by supporting the local rebellions against Napoleon's move of installing his brother Josef on the Spanish Throne. At this point in time Nathan R, had travelled to England and got initially involved in the textile business and had already in his possession an unknown amount of funds from the Prince of the Hessian's Treasure at his disposal.

In order to support Wellington's military efforts as now a British subject he desperately needed cash for the Gold Purchase and here I believe that the LOAN" from the Prince of Hessian came handy. Napoleon's effective blockade of English Merchant ships, with the help of his Corsican friends, made it risky to do the transport at sea so the fact that his French brother who was conducting finance business in Paris, became part of the solution.

Now the way the British Army in Portugal and Spain had managed to pay for their supplies was by "trading" the "checks" drafted on the British Ministry of Finance (The Exchequers Office) and through the Bank of England, was by "selling" them at a very high discounted rate (up to 50%).

Nathan Rothschild knew this as he had purchased the papers (checks) at the end of the line in London and somehow ended up making heavy profits on these deals. These "papers" had been made available to him from the efforts of the commissioners from a paper trade company (discounting of government backed drafts or checks called CAB, which was obtained from an unholy alliance of a Group of Spanish, Sicilian and Malthesian Bankers. The French R-branch was also getting hold of these discounted checks; through their agents.

So far the Rothschild's English branch had made profit 2 major ways: on the same type of business:

ONE: By buying and selling the Gold from the East Indian Trading company, and then selling the Gold to the British Government with an undisclosed profit. These bars had been sold to the British Government that was now faced with a problem: How to get them to Spain safe and sound as the

French had an effective blockade going on; on the Seaways.

TWO: By buying and selling of the Wellington drafts.

The last way of doing business came up as an "opportunity" to solve the transport problem of the Gold. This opportunity the R's grabbed with eagerness, as they now could use their network of built-up secret or confidential agents in Holland, Germany and even France to exchange French coins for British Gold. So the set-up was clear; to transport this money by many hands and by different roads to the Wellington Army, that made it now possible to advance as they then could pay for their local supplies. The story does not tell if any of the money from selling supplies and arms (weapons) ended up in any of the R's coffers via cohorts. I have to show cautious imagination in connection with this last potential scenario. What we know was that the preferred mode of transportation was false bottom wagons.

So at last **a third way** to make money on this international situation called the Napoleonic wars was to make commissions by exchanging the Gold into French franc. (Someone with a higher integrity may call this a treasonous act if there is such a thing when it comes to ways of earning money!)

As a definitely unknown way to make money the 4th way was to provide certain “hard money” to obtain and sell military supplies. But that could result in being shot out of a French canon! From both sides for the conflict but this way of conducting business was to set precedence for similar transactions in the future.

As a reminder this is how the Duchy of Hessen had made or conducted business with the English during the American revolutionary war. They rented out professional soldiers and officers in Union Jack uniform that only spoke German. The movie, “the Patriot” with Mel Gibson as the main actor, is a powerful historical presentation of that scenario.

The British got some money back when the Hessians received the dead bodies back as they paid by the number of coffins returned; A quirk of faith?

So here was a blueprint for making money from buying and selling government assets or papers to arrange loans for weaponry in times of war! What other business was untouched –you tell me as my imagination don't stretch that far. THE BASIC MORAL OF THAT TRUE STORY COULD BE: START UP YOUR BUSINESS WITH OTHER PEOPLES (GOVERNMENTS—collected via Taxation) MONEY: THEN SPEND "YOUR OWN" WISELY.

The Records shows that the way Nathan Rothschild could get into that much money via the Hessian Treasury that he could pay(cash) for the Indian Gold and then sell it to the English, is to find from the War Scene annals as well. In 1776, the Hessian Duchy had participated in the American Revolution with rented soldiers to the British.

They may or may not have indirectly been involved in the Civil War after the botched up Marxist revolution in 1849, in Prussia. A number of the revolutionaries from that revolt fled to Chicago and a decade later "participated" in the Yankee Army according to informed sources. This information was unearthed from my stay in the "deep South". The Confederate Treasurer fled the other way back to England when the outcome of that conflict became clear. Was Mr. Benjamin Judah a British finance agent? Sorry for this digression!

What was at stake as Napoleons generals were campaigning in Germany after certain guidelines? Prince de Talleyrand, the grey Eminence and the Secretary of Foreign affairs may have worked out this strategy in council with his mysterious mentors. Only Bayern, Baden, Württemberg and Prussia, typical city states, was to get support from the French Emperor and become part of the "Rhine-Verband";(An alliance that had been drawn up by the Secretary of Foreign Affairs!?)

So when the Prince of Hessen was forced to flee overnight and take refuge with family in the Danish Royal Courts, the Rothschild patriarch Maier Amschel suddenly found himself in power as I have stated. He had at that time obtained the function of trusted lender of government loans and controlled after the departure of the Prince most of the assets in the Treasury. A greater part of this money had come from the rental of

Hessian soldiers that was employed as officers in the Union Jack Army in the War of American Independence. This was of course a new deal of the olden times system of hiring out mercenaries, as from the Viking rebel colony of the Joms Vikings. Quite a career jump! The clever man from the Jewish ghetto in Juden Strasse in Frankfurt had made his way up in life from being an odd fellow with the knowledge of chess and rare coins and way up the ladder to the position of external financial advisor for the Princes of Hessian. Actually he had climbed even higher as he had started out as a junk collector and dealer in used merchandize.

One of his debtors at the time of the Napoleonic thrust for control of Europe was the Austrian-Hungarian Empire. He had wisely already set up his next oldest son, Solomon in business in Vienna.

Nobody really knows how much money was collected by Maier Amschel and his sons that ended up covering: England, France, Austria-Hungary and Italy in addition to Germanic City states and Duchy's with state loans. What we know is that a larger sum made its way back to England and as with a whim of fate I believe that this is how Nathan got the money to buy the "Ost-Indian" Gold, and that made it possible for the family to acquire the most golden edged papers on the London Stock Exchange. This is my final presentation or preparation to the next chapters in this amazing family's route to unlimited power and that ended up controlling I would say most of the wealth in Europe and later other places. If you had an option of becoming the King or the director of a "national bank", which position would provide you with the most power? The answer to this question was becoming obvious.

CHAPTER FOUR: THE ULTIMATE STING OPERATION.

It may also have been the final strike towards unlimited controlling influence over the economy of an empire on decline: The British Monarchy. And again the main player that would be the impetuous cause and making it possible was again the ambitious French "Alexander the Great"; by his presence on the scene of history made unprecedented opportunities possible.

The final and famous battle of Napoleons waterloo is a subject of controversy with an ungodly assembly of backers you are not supposed to clarify for therein lies the clue open to what happened in the sinister part of the financial world today. My presentation in this book on alternative economical systems may have historical flaws and disagreements as the subject is as controversial as can be. About twenty plus years of research has been zoomed in on pieces of the puzzle, and when I thought I had "nailed it", though ere was another puzzle behind the first puzzle and so on. Welcome to the world of a historical researcher into the glum world of international finance. Somehow the idea that if you knew the past it was going to be easier to predict the future may be fallacy. It may be a corollarary of if you "find the truth it will set you free." Along the way I had my epiphanies and more than once I have been baffled with the ingenuity of some of these plots of obtaining control of the "Golden Pot." Man's ambitions are sometimes inextricable to the degree of what means they are willing to use and justify in the process.

An ambitious statement however; I cannot see it otherwise and need to tell as I was privy to almost finding out a pattern in the final battle of my own assets as a researcher, Human Rights Commission Chairman and business consultant. My Human Rights work and research prompted my interest in diving into more sources than I can count from and at first my exposure of hidden strategies in upper Law Enforcement during the Nazi occupational authority was a "trip".

It amazes me to what length officials are willing to go to protect their own inequities through cover-ups; as was orchestrated by the Third Reich. This includes classifying files for a long time period as 75 years. The only real reason for this that I can think of is to hide certain individual actions.

At the tail end of my stay in my country of birth I ran into, in the very last days before moving to the free world, a very private group that no one had even heard of in the library community which should have records of any organization that operated on the country's soil. By the grace of God I was lead to a major piece in this puzzle in a library of UCLA; half the global circumference away in the posh neighborhood of Beverly Hills; two years later. I was looking for another reference in order to get closure in another matter that had caught my attention the previous years. That constellation is off the subject and I will not bring this matter to the plate at this sitting—probably never. In that same section of shelving, that I was lead over to, I found by an immediate glance what turned out to be a numbered publication that obviously had belonged to a member of this more than mysterious organization or private club. In retrospect it may and have slipped the attention of the librarian back in my country of birth as the subject was as plausible as the word "The Travelers Club" and may have been sorted under a different heading than organization. I can say it was not a publication related to the subject of tourism—at least that would be a longest stretch I can think of, however it showed on the limited pages of this type of pamphlet; the who is who of whom are 'TRAVELING" IN THE CIRCUIT OR

CIRCLES OF INTERNATIONAL POLITICAL FINANCE." From the time we are dealing with—the aftermath of the Napoleonic Area. As it is being realized in recent years; the money is senior to politics.

Established in a year just past the incarceration of Napoleon at Elba, the "club" had been endorsed by the Prince of Wales and The Duke of Wellington as an honorary member. Both had given additional credibility to the validity of such a private organization. My question is how come this private club with the innocent name as "The Travelers Club" enjoyed the most secret secrecy of any organization I have heard of in my long career as a researcher? The obvious question is what were they hiding?

Well the fact that Prince De Talleyrand, the most versatile politician in French or European politics was one of the main members, and I would say provocateurs give one clue of its shady undertakings. He must have been born in secrecy and would of course operate on a secret agent basis in and out of 3 or 4 different French governments before Napoleon's. He was the man that paved the way for the negotiations in Vienna with all important political dignitaries present in the days while Napoleon was sitting incarcerated and before he made "another run for office." One of his specialties during the important Vienna conference was to make sure the head of nations and other VIP's was accompanied to their rooms with sophisticated floozies that would gather secrets for the now minister with "*no portefouile*". He would also decipher letter-imprints from the surface of the table cover where the attending ministers wrote their letters. These obtained secrets he would use during the negotiations of the future of Europe, which would benefit the new world of finance.

The hundred days of Napoleon's comeback had come down to the final battle where Prussia had joined the English, to stop the crazy dictator who had in his insane rush for Russia lost half a million men, many of which were just boys 14-15 years old. So the Prussian General Blucher and Wellington were clashing against the vestiges of the former so powerful Army of the dictator mounted on his white horse.

Nathan Rothschild was actually following the action from his horse on a remote hill and when it was obvious how it was going to end he went on a beeline to "Ostende" by the channel. It was stormy weather on the channel and the wave action rougher than any skipper would agree to risk ship and life to engage in to carry him over to Dover. The wind was too powerful for the pigeons to fly—they were all grounded so the only way to get message about the by now crucial outcome by the French dictator battle, was to bring oneself across somehow. Nathan R found a man willing to risk both of their lives against a substantial pay and Nathan landed In Dover before daybreak where he had his carriage waiting. On the dot for the opening of the London Stock Exchange he was at his regular pillar leaning nonchalantly with one of the most famous poker-faces planted on his shoulders. The man was known for not showing any emotions or "batting an eye" in dealing and wheeling in money transactions.

The moment had come and he was ready to play probably the most lucrative game of his life. Nathan R had a network of loyal agents on the floor buying stocks and bonds that were dumped at extremely discounted rates and the other players followed suit with what Mr. Rothschild himself was selling and buying. He was dealing his chips as if the little Frenchman had won the battle. So the whole London finance world followed suit and Nathan R's efforts to "limit" losses as well by selling out short while the share values plummeted as a goose trying to cross the channel in that awful weather. It was not until later in that morning when it was known the outcome of the Blucher/Wellington coalition had actually defeated Napoleon once and for all. At that point Nathan R had reversed all his plays.

How much money that was lost for the majority of "investors" if not all of the gamblers is not known! How much money the R's won that day on the Stock-exchange is not known either but it may have been enough to get the upper hand in English Finance –and control of the Bank of England? A brilliant man that if he had used his forte towards benign means could have placed his name in the annals of the great humanitarian benefactors! The moral of this story I can't tell you but a system where you can make huge sums of money by just shuffling papers and which took precedence in a lot of Stock-Exchanges across the new world after that set precedence for monetary schemes and greedy profits with no real production and here is where finance clashes with an honest and productive economy.

CHAPTER FIVE: "FAMILY" BUSINESS AT BEST.

The catalyzing factor and the men behind Napoleon!

The French revolution may have had its upspring among the peasants and the commoners, however the actual plot was to dislodge the position of the French Monarch, as he was a typical proponent of ridiculous spending from the Royal Treasury chest –which was a social concern as well of course. His predecessor Louis the XIV, also known as the Sun-king, had disarmed the population in terms of tax contributions and lavishly spent money on Versailles, the famous royal abode with mirrors covering the main ballroom from floor to ceiling as a quirk of vanity at best. The gardens behind the castle were laid out with no end in sight; I visited the Versailles in 1977; in connection with a human rights conference. My thoughts were reluctantly going back to the guillotine-party after a later king that was in power up to the revolution; why was it was necessary to execute him! By the way, I don't think the joke of why Frenchmen are shorter than most Europeans being that so many of them were guillotined, is very funny.

What was happening in the prelude of this so-called revolution of the peasants and the famous attack on the Bastille that functioned as the royal prison and that had incarcerated the most rebellious protester to and of the Royal waste and thus undue taxation? Through taxation was the only way the monarchs and money to spend, unless you do like Prince Charles and start your own fruit and vegetable operation on vacant land or "unproductive" land. The situation in France was ripe for an under-handed plot which started fifteen years earlier in the south east region of the Germanic patchwork of Duchy's and city states.

The historical person of Adam Weisshaupt, Professor at the Ingolstadt University, a man that was described as blacker than a black sheep, infiltrated the Jesuit organization on his own volition or as part of an unholy consortium, with the purpose of breaking down their structure that was known of being behind the 2nd Renaissance in Europe.

As spiritual consultants to the Royalties these men from the Ignatius Loyola Monasteries, had been banned by the pope already in the 1730-ties. They succeeded in talking the Royalties into investing from the Royal Treasury Chests in different forms of art schools including music, theater and fine art in general for the enlightenment of the people, and thus spearheading a 2nd Renaissance in Europe.

The Jesuits could easily see through this man and when all attempts to bring him around or convert him failed they banned him and threw him out of their organization as a black sheep that could not be converted! This man's next escapade came about when he surfaced as the founder of the Illuminati Organization in the crucial year of 1776. He was to play a major role in reorganizing the upper levels of the original Germanic FREE-masonry. When he was going for his next ambition to recruit the French chapters from the Duke of Orleans into this new system that advocated Reason with no religious over-tones, one of his messengers was struck by lightning from his horse when travelling through the black forest in Bayern.

This man was found by the Gendarmes' of the Bayern Monarchy and baffled by the scrolled subversive writings he was "carrying" on his body and they declared Adam Weisshaupt as a persona non-grata and he had to flee.

The early beginning of the "reincarnation" of the secret system that played out in the courts of King Solomon, considered by many adherents to be the first Master Mason, has ascribed the building of the famous Solomon's Temple to the secret beginnings. Hiram Abiff the Phoenician King, and architectural builder was recorded having sacrificed his life when tested to give away obvious secrets connected to the architectural master work. When leaving the city of Jerusalem on his way back to Tyre he had been stopped by the workers on the temple inside the walls of Jerusalem.

They wanted to have some questions answered about "the origin of that temple", I believe. There were four gates to and from the City of Jerusalem, one of each of the main compass-directions. At the last gate he made a run for it and was slain and thus the Secrets were kept for posterity. Hiram Abiff, an initiate, has been upheld as an elated example of one that was able to keep the secrets even when faced with death.

The official year of establishing the free-mason system inspired by the apprenticeship system of the stone masons that is responsible for magnificent cathedrals across Europe, of which just one was the Cathedral of Cologne. These builders were referred to as Free-Masons as they just needed to show their "union-card" and not any other type of national identity card when they crossed the borders within the Holy Roman Empire for another Cathedral-job.

The re-inception of the new "free-masons" not having any connection to any stone builder organization was actually a protest movement from the "bourgeois" that started secret meetings where they could free their thoughts from the influence of the Holy Roman Church.

At the time of Adam Weisshaupt the upper level of their organization welcomed these new levels of the illuminati-enlightenment, as dissatisfaction and stagnation had entered the minds of the members.

But not all went for this coup of their organization; a Scottish scholar, from the University of Edinburg rejected the invitation to join in this new framework. He was very suspicious of these "new" levels and started warning fellah masons about this attempt to coup and derailing their system from 1717. His name Joseph Robison, wrote an exhaustive report on the involvement of this new faction in the aftermath of the French Revolution just a few years after it took place.(in 1797) The book is called "A proof of conspiracy" and was republished in paperback as a classic in the US in 1967. Tough but worthwhile reading!

NOTE: History doesn't always give you the right picture of historical events, an understatement, as it is usually written by the victorious factions of any conflict. This is definitely the case with the French Revolution, of 1789. It was of course not easy to see the actual plot behind the stage at the time, and the development of other historical events would take place before the real picture was clear.

The Bavarian Police from this Kingdom north of the Alps, had found a messenger obviously struck from his horse after a lightning strike in the black forest. Again the secret roll or scroll they found on his body and its content had Adam Weisshaupt declared persona non grata and subsequently a fugitive. He disappeared from the scene and resurfaced soon after with new financial backing?

The paperwork as said was intended a Masonic dignitary as the Duke of Orleans, and was subversive in content to the degree that the Royal Establishment of Bavaria was up in arms about this new organization that was being cooped by this Illuminati faction of the accepted free-masonry.

But Illuminati resurfaced with a strengthened financial backing and new paper scrolls outlining a coup against a vulnerable Monarchy that was intercepted by a member of the Vatican Clergy that rushed to the Holy Seat/Sea to report the findings.

At this point the Jacobiner faction of the Holy Church in Paris was already contaminated. (The

Jacobiners was the friars of the same order as Thomas of Aquinas and not the Franciscan order)

The infringement on the Catholic Church in Paris complicated business as in the Holy Roman factional control of the French Monarchy. (inherent in the term Holy Roman Empire when the Church qualified who was going to be the King from the different countries, and went to the excess to Crown a few of them. The French King was toppled and we know what happened in the wake; three different governments before the infamous dictator Napoleon paved the way for a coup and dictatorial ruling of France and with aspirations to control Europe. One man that is mentioned above was the Secretary of Foreign Affairs; Prince de Talleyrand that had "survived" in that position throughout the previous governments and after the fall of his mentor or protégé from the "throne" had to continue his political and worse machinations "underground". This is where I found him Instrumental in one of the most secret European international organization from a publicly displaced booklet in the UCLA-University Library in 1987; Along with dignitaries as the Duke of Wellington and the

Prince of Wales on the "advisory board". This was most likely an enactment probably for the sake of having an internal impeccable front with the purpose of recruitment of strategically placed and loyal recruits.

CHAPTER SIX: FUTURE FINANCIAL CONTROL.

The absence of the Royal family somehow didn't fly with the French population. By popular demand after the travesty of the Napoleonic Era, they had to be brought back though with no real influence of the money supply or financing of the French state. The royalties now had mainly assumed a PR-function and the institution had somehow a calming influence on the people.

The Vatican was in financial problems I believe due to the de-embarkation of the Monarchial Treasury Chest, and it wasn't until late 1820-ties before they were graced by the first loan by a French consortium of 6 lenders of which I believe the French R-rep was the instrumental coordinator. This coordinative backing may have lasted up until the Mussolini-alliance with Hitler.

The take-over of political (read financial) power in France and moving into position and call the "shots".

In Vienna-Austria and England there was a definite shift of power, but it wasn't until 1900 with the establishing of the Socialist Revolutionary organization surfaced in Switzerland that the moving and shaking of the subject of "Why was the Monarchy necessary," when someone else could control the money supply across the borders and call it "the financial system."

A number of political assassinations at first directed at the Tsar Regime in Russia already in the 1870-ties and with the culmination of the assassination-liquidation of the whole Tsar family (1919) took the "wind" out of the sails for the opposition. And the playing field was now totally open and ripe for the first Bolshevik regime; and thus the communist Empire was cemented in the former proud Russian Tsar regime.

But before this happened, the WWI would have to come to a closure and the participants "to have gone home." WWI exhausted all the troops involved but can be traced back to a conflict between Serbia and Bulgaria in 1911 or 3 years before the official historical kick-off of this European conflict.

Throughout the history of our planet conflicts has arisen as someone or some group had a purpose for this to happen; I believe which is contradictory to what a university professor has been taught.

The Arch Duke or the last heir to the Austrian-Hungarian Empire was shot off his horse back on a peace mission to the Balkan Peninsula. However this was three years after the Bulgarians were pushed back, and after Romania failed in a similar way. The fearless warriors of Serbia could not be beaten and when the Austrian-Hungarian Empire got involved and was losing ground, that is when Prussia started to move and the infamous shots in Sarajevo was instigated.(By a zealot from a base in Switzerland?)

Before this happened in 1914, a whole evolution of eradicating Monarchies had taken place. The assassination of the King Ludwig of Bavaria was the end of that Monarchy: the assassination of King Umberto the First and the 2nd wiped out the Italian Monarchy; and King George of Greece was killed in 1913! The French withstood an attempt on the royalties, but most European Kingdoms was gone but “political” access to the finances of these countries had now been opened up.

After WWI, the six Monarchies of the Balkan’s had been replaced with Yugoslavia.

There is no secret today? that these assaults on the Monarchies and indirectly the control of the Treasury Chests was orchestrated through this Socialist Revolutionary organization that was cleverly organized as to who or what group was to pull the strings via a Russian engineer that turned out to work for the Tsar’s secret Police of Ohkraina or as a plant inside that organization. His exposure along with a publisher in the Germanic Territory more or less dissolved that early organization about the year of 1909? At least it had to be reorganized to pull off the last part of the strategy; to remove more royalties away from controlling the Treasure Chest.

Power control of the money is a ruthless game as evidenced when the wife of the Austrian-Hungarian Emperor was seeking consultation in her grief over having lost her children. After her consultation with the host at the Geneva Lake resort of a powerful finance family, she was assassinated on the way back to her Geneva hotel. She was travelling incognito cloaked with a hooded cape and had expressed her frustration and grief in the consultation.

As an Afterword to this chapter it is interesting to state the word from the matriarch of the R'S, when she was interviewed on her birthday when she was way into her nineties": "It is up to my boys (her five sons) whether or not we're going to have a war!"

I interpret this statement according to how their business with government loans across Europe was conducted, that only her sons could release the money-loans that made it possible to buy the weapons for warfare. One can ask if there was any morality in such a statement or not. If you supply money for weapons you are not the one that pulls the trigger—of course. However if you supply the weapons necessary to conduct war I believe that is a different issue; but I am not stating that was the case:

> As mentioned and now reiterated; the European political landscape was totally changed at the end of WWI, Monarchies had

gone left and right to never be fully re-established including the 6 monarchies of the Balkans.

The Kingdom of Bavaria was gone already before the year of 1900; the Alberto 1rst and 2nd of Italy had been assassinated and that was the end of the Italian Monarchy. King George of Greece had been assassinated in 1913, a year before the last heir to the Austrian –Hungarian Empire was assassinated in Sarajevo in 1914. I believe this trace back to the fact that Serbia was very successful in defending themselves against aggression originally from Bulgaria. The instigators of this conflict are hidden in the fog that dimmed plots that may have been originated from the vast territory of Russia. Was the Balkan monarchies considered a threat to financial dominance over Europe?

After WWI was over and done with the last huge piece of the getting rid of the Monarchial influential puzzle; the Tsar Regime, was soon to become history and replaced by one of the most viscous and lasting Dictatorships of modern times. Their specialty was dealing in secrecy and plot against the Intellectuals and others that didn't get along with the new doctrines; by deporting them to the labor camps in Siberia for "re-indoctrination."

I HAVE TOUCHED ON THE EVOLUTION FOR PAVING THE WAY FOR THE "GREATEST HUMAN EXPERIMENT", AS STATED BY A FAMOUS PSYCHOLOGIST. The Evolution started inside Russia and lead to the establishment of the secret Police of the Tsar called Ohkraina. The name may have or not been focusing on the landscape of Ukraine as the bread-basket of Russia. There was of course subversive elements in Russia, the largest Kingdom not counting the Chinese Dynasties.

This part of Europe stretching from the Ural Mountain chain in the east and to the Atlantics was separating the continent from the immense Asian part called Siberia has a fairly short history compared to the Southern regions. This northern part of Europe was in old History books referred to as Svidjod and has been shrouded in a lot of Mythology or Mystery.

The main Seat of the Founder OR ORGANIZING OF THIS TERRITORY the mythological figure of Odin was to have come out of the Aral Mountains and set up court just north of the area that was much later referred to as Venice of Norden, Stockholm. A lake north of Stockholm called Sigtuna was the main seat that later moved further north to Uppsala, a major University today.

The Mongolian terror by the name of Genghis Kahn had claimed major part of Svidjod under his command.—he was actually controlling a territory that was 4 times as large as the hey-days of the Roman Empire. He ended the old Norse Viking settlements; the settlements of Gardarrike (meaning the Kingdom of farms and that had its main seat in Kiev of Ukraine) and Varangia, that had cleared forests further east and North of the Kazhar Kingdom by the Black Sea.

Russia though, enjoyed several hundred years of uninterrupted Monarchial Rule, where the peasants had altogether an autonomous position in the communes that was established by the Norse settlers.

This historical fact is of importance as these communes consisted of settlers of cleared land that decided to work together by arranging their agricultural plots around a circular or elliptic plaza where their abodes were located up front. Their plots went as far back as needed to support the residents of these communes with provisions. There were certain skilled “mechanics” in the black-smith industry, the horse-shoeing business and the making of leather clothes from animal skins, and other specialties that had been taking care of the farmers from olden times in the countries within the Nordic territories. These early Russian communes were a vital improvement of coordinating not only the necessities of life but also their social structure. This commune system worked very well in terms of bartering or exchanging products so everyone’s need was taken care of, and thus became a blueprint of a successful system of “communism.”

The communist revolutionaries actually ran into remnants of this workable system of early economics when they expanded their gradual control of the Russian Empire eastward.

It took several years before Russia was fully under the totalitarian yoke of the Bolsheviks (originally a minority political Party as the Mensheviks was the majority party consisting of members of the successful agricultural communities.)

There will always be critical voices towards the small group in power as I would say others would like to usurp that power for themselves.

The larger the country the bigger the cherry to grab by the plotters and these were dealt with in development areas as the Siberia during the Tsar Regime. Hard work has from time memorial not really hurt anybody, and the plan was to make these revolutionary rebels come to their senses and be integrated back into the Russian Society. However, the botched Marxist Revolution in Prussia from 1849 lead to deporting and escape I would say to the East and to the Chicago Area (where these rebels came to play a decisive role within the Yankee Army and the outcome of the Civil War in the US—this statement is totally mine.)

The ones that "landed" in Russia were instrumental in paving the way for a change of regime, thus the establishing of the Secret Police of the Tsar Ohkraina. It is noteworthy to remark that the exterior branch of the Scotland Yard was established the same year as Ohkraina in 1881. There was a family connection between the Tsars and the British Monarchy.

Several tough characters managed to escape the labor camps and ad byways found their way to Geneva Switzerland from where they became part of an organization called the Socialist Revolutionaries established in the year of 1900. Missions of no returns were launched towards the Tsar Government. These men and women were to be considered anarchists; Zealots that was ready to sacrifice their lives for the Cause. Their main targets were politicians, police commissioners and the Royal Family. The police-inspector Phleve in St. Petersburg was one of their victims. Their favorite MO was home-made bombs that were detonated on their bodies when throwing themselves in front of a carriage as an official procession went by. They were waiting for the right moment and from strategic position in the crowd they rushed out when the procession went by. Today we would recognize this as actions from a suicide bomber.

There was a revolutionary attempt from the group in St Petersburg in 1905 that was lead by

Vladimir Lenin and that was botched. Lenin and others managed to flee and took on London as their new stomping ground. A Scotland Yard man, Reginald Howe, that was to become the chairman of the revitalized Interpol Executive Committee (1946), was hiding in a closet where intelligence had told Scotland Yard that a rebel rouse meeting was going to be held with the barbers of London; a feeding ground for more recruits. He got himself installed in the space ahead of the meeting and through a crack in a closet he got a good look at the reincarnated devil himself and his oratorical abilities. At some point police-inspector Reginald Howe was knighted to Sir by the British Monarch.

Meanwhile the plot against the Royal Treasury Golden Pot continued across Europe and when the stage for WWI was set, which was expediently blamed on the Serbians, three years after the fact of its evolution, there was only one player left as an obstacle for total control of the European Finance Constellations; and that was the Tsarist Russia.

At the end of the stale dated world-war it was time for a successful revolution; the October or

Bolshevik Revolution of 1917. Lenin showed up with a new group of revolutionaries from Geneva and money that passed or was guided through Germany on their way to St Petersburg in that reported "blacked out train." Here they met Leon Trotsky the second of command. Trotsky had gone from Switzerland or London as a journalist to New York. In New York he rallied support from 200 exiled comrades and they embarked on the Steamship "Kristiania", from New York via Halifax with the New York revolutionaries on board. In Halifax, Canada, they broke into military facilities and stole Canadian surplus uniforms and headed for the rendezvous with Lenin in St Petersburg. The grayish-blue uniforms with added distinctions became their PR-front in times to come. Again let's face it; you can't really conduct a revolution without zealots, money and weapons. Further you need a strategy: Lenin's was besides liquidating as many objectioner's as possible, was fairly simple. Control of the water-front; take over the railroads and all communications. That was the radio network and the newspapers. Most people my age will remember "The Pravda", which means "the Truth" of course.

By traversing the railroad along the western part of the country and their reinforced locomotives (armored and equipped with canons and machineguns just in case they would run into opposition). This is how they took control of one railroad city after the other; all the way to the Black Sea. How big was the Army of these revolutionary rebels?: Actually just short of a thousand. Meanwhile the majority of the residents of the Russian landscape were not affected in the beginning. But slowly and surely and by installing loyal commissioners along the way, and confiscating farms and private land they gradually took control over the whole Russia. The white Russians that had sworn allegiance to the Tsar was eventually defeated and disillusioned when the whole Tsar family along with the kids were executed in Ekatharinaburg (named after Katharina the great) on the slopes of the Aral Mountains. The Tsar's Army had been decimated in the German WWI conflict and there is a rumor that the Army officers had been rooted out by soldiers that was supporters of the revolution against the Tsar.

We are all familiar with the accounts of Alexander Solchenitskin of how the power was consolidated in this former so proud empire.

The information about the existence of the Socialist Revolutionary organization with headquarter in Geneva Switzerland we may credit a Russian co-revolutionary; Boris Savinkov, who wrote a book after it was clear in his mind that the secret agenda of the revolution was not something a decent human being would ever support. He had been one of Lenin's closest supporters, but when several of his buddies had been executed by the communist leaders he managed to smuggle his manuscript out of Russia and to France where it was translated. Boris Savinkov was executed as well.

I read excerpt of his account in the Norwegian literary Magazine "Arken" in 1985, at the time I where studying political constellations around WWI I and had reached an impasse.

Since this is a book on historical economics I have to mention that the infamous famine in Ukraine in the early twenties came about in that area where the Norsemen had established agricultural farmland a thousand years earlier.

Ukraine was later considered to be the bread basket of Russia and became the place for the hoarding or confiscation of food that created a famine that decimated several millions Ukrainians. With the intervention of the League of Nations (pre-runner to the United Nations) and where Fritof Nansen, the Norwegian explorer and humanitarian with the military-man Vidkun Quisling as next in command was running the aid-expedition that may have in the process re-established the transport lines and so inadvertently may have saved that part of the food distribution system for the communist empire?

So this was a cursory introduction into the sometimes dismal or gloomy world of; International finance. I think it was important to pull some of those rabbit out of the hole and enlighten my audience in the process. These rabbits were more sinister and more wolverine-like and complicated than the regular kind and they were not addicted to carrots.

I do sincerely hope that I have presented a carrot for my audience and that this initial extensive introduction to historical finance will jive the weather-hairs for the next part of my presentation.

The next Part will concentrate on Economics more than Finance and I will clearly show the difference and hopefully bring enlightenment on that subject as well. For the heck of it I may even ask you to read my dissertation on Chicko-nomics or Chicken-Economics that should be available real soon. As a bona-fide chicken farmer for seven long years (retirement years) I feel confident in forwarding my knowledge on this subject as well. And who knows reading and studying that subject may inspire you to establish your own Chicken-coop; for economical reasons.

Meanwhile, while I'm putting pieces together from the full manuscript I wrote on the main subject (the Golden Pot) 18 years ago, after I had consulted the general business community for 20 years, I wish you productive days of good production and cope with the current economical/financial situation as best as you can.

Truly and Sincerely Yours:
Trygve Gangnaes Jr, San Francisco August 2015.

AFTERMATH:

More than a note: What baffles a bystander and what may prevent full understanding of international political finance may be why the democratic process "has to be bypassed!" In a country where there are no Monarchs in the way the target seems to be the "elected" president. The killing or assassination of President William McKinley, I believe is a total mystery still, though it did happen during the terror reign of the Swiss Anarchists! Before that there were at least three attempts on American Presidents of which two was a success. The one that failed was on President Andrew Jackson (there was actually two attempts of misfiring!) What did he do that antagonized the int. finance elite?: That one is clear cut: He "killed the bank" by his own words and he spent a major part of his second term to stop that twenty-year bank charter that was up for renewal in 1836. This 20-years Charter that may have been a compromise was originally signed by the first President George Washington back in 1791, and was due for renewal in 1811. It was voted out and that was maybe the reason for the new warring conflict with England. It was renewed again 4 years later in New Orleans in 1916. General Andrew Jackson was part of the truce signing in Louisiana.

Abraham Lincoln was an admirer of Andrew Jackson. He had his portrait hanging by the fireplace in the oval office. I believe he was killed when he refused to obtain loans at interest with the English finance agents. As we remember Lincoln decided to release money at zero percent interest. The money referred to is "the greenbacks." British Finance Agents, and as we all know was bypassed when Lincoln decided to use the treasury to handle the financing of paying material suppliers and the rebuilding after the civil war. The bill was close to 300 million dollars at the time.

After his demise a policy of double backing of the money let out in circulation; in Gold and Silver, was referred to as the bi-metallic backing system. Lo and Behold when this system was challenged and President Garfield wanted to uphold it—"it seems as he had to be assassinated!!" As I and quite a few others see it;

the combination of Gold and Silver is more flexible that just the Gold as there is more of Silver and thus can't that easily be manipulated or speculated with. There was already an act in force from the early 1870-ties that introduced this combined backing of the currency distributed: in gold and silver.

This of course reminds me and others of the executive directive of John F Kennedy of June 1963; that reintroduced the right of the citizens to go to the bank with the paper bill dollar and obtain a silver dollar. That sounded too good to be true and it was, however I laid my eyes on one of these silver certificates from 1964. President Nixon, John F's contester to the Presidency in 1959-election later paved the way for abandoning the gold Standard all together.

In retrospect I realize that I'm handling explosive information in this write-up of: "The Plot against the Golden Pot." It is a huge subject or undertaking and I have most likely only sketched out the tip of this icy world called international finance. "Why can't we all get along" with what we can obtain as productive citizens and in pursuit of the happiness we are entitled to. One major consolation in all this and is that according to "Genesis" the first book of the holy bible, we are born in the image of God and as such we are spiritual beings and not in the flesh as we have been told and that we may become free from financial intrigues next time around. Our grand-children may or may not have to pay that enormous debt that the framers of the constitution and Presidents like Jefferson, Jackson and Lincoln to name a few was warning us about.

I will rest my case here; however if time and health allows me I will present a multitude of alternative systems that has proven workable from our past; when it comes to real economics! I may just start that (ad)venture with an introduction to Chicken-Economics which was run by me, years ago as a successful blog.

Thank you and good night.

Made in the USA
Monee, IL
04 November 2026

67385492R00036